The QA Advantage

Written by:
Michael Pasono

Contents

4

Overview

Summary

The QA Advantage provides the reader with Quality Assurance methods that provide your existing business or startup with quality-related competitive advantages.

This book will showcase the key subjects of quality assurance and quality engineering. We take a proactive and strategic approach that will lay out quality assurance subject areas, key descriptions, purpose, impacts to revenue if not implemented, and positive or negative real-world results.

Key subject areas within this book include the following:

- Test Strategy
- Test Management
- Increasing Test Maturity
- Quality Improvement Process
- Service Virtualization Testing
- Database Virtualization
- DevOps QA
- Quality Revenue Impacts

About the Author

Michael Pasono is the author behind the titled books: <u>The QA Advantage; Software Testing Series; Identity and Data Protection for the Average Person</u> who systematically lays out the different areas and concepts of Quality Assurance, Software Engineering, Innovation, Data Protection, and Software Testing to assure right level of quality is applied at the right time.

Technology is continuing to evolve at a rapid pace, these educational books are meant to familiarize yourself with key software testing concepts and position yourself for the completive advantage.

Michael's professional experience and advocacy in systems quality improvement have him recognized as an industry leader in technology innovations and assuring high-quality systems leveraging real-world experiences.

Michael shares key quality topics and recommends approaches to assure a high-quality product is being produced. The recommendations are provided by Michael and not any paid sponsors or previous employers.

Why Important

The QA Advantage book was written to help educate on ways to utilize quality assurance practices to gain a competitive advantage.

As technology advances rapidly, advanced software quality assurance methods are needed to assure proper software quality to keep or attract more consumers of your product or service.

Innovation and a growth mindset must be driven in your company culture to gain the competitive advantage you need.

Your company values need to reflect your aspiration for being the best product or service in your industry.

Companies

Large companies are modernizing their technology at a rapid pace to keep up with consumer expectations of an always-on product or service. Companies are taking on new challenges such as digital transformations and cloud migrations.

Not only are these large-scale changes occurring, but ongoing new threats are also appearing more rapidly. These threats are around cybersecurity and data privacy. Board members, shareholders, and CEOs need to address to reduce risk.

With companies collecting so much data as it provides more value, they have to hire quality experts to keep this technology humming and data safe to assure their brand reputation and stay in business. Those of you in the quality assurance and control areas need to stay current or even ahead of these changes coming.

Quality Management Umbrella

Quality management practices have been around for decades. This concept is having a systematic approach to assure processes and control quality testing has transitioned from manufacturing into engineering. This series will cover topics from both Quality Assurance, Engineering, and Quality Control best practices.

Here is a quick overview of the difference. This is a key area to understand before moving into the series.

Quality Assurance is all about setting up the process in which to conduct quality control. Think of it as an umbrella over most testing activities execution. This explanation has helped guide the path to identifying wherein the development life-cycle this quality topic falls into.

Quality Control is about the execution of processes defined in Quality Assurance. Testing heavily falls under the control section.

Many executives interchange Quality Assurance with Testing-only activity. This is a false pretense and this book should debunk that notion of equality and help you educate the proper roles.

Software Development

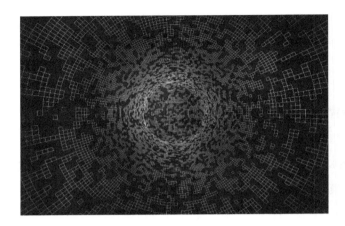

Software testing has a great deal of interaction with how software should be developed and tested.

Software development has rapidly evolved over the years making changes to quality assurance methods.

This book goes over many areas of the software development and testing lifecycle such as requirements to implementation into production and applies key quality assurance and control best practices, along with introducing new advanced and modern techniques.

Key subjects and topics in this book are meant to be an introduction and not a full advanced playbook on how to implement. Please continue to educate yourself on any key areas you find interesting or think could provide further quality-related improvements to your organization.

Chapter 1 – What is a Test Strategy

Definitions

What is a test strategy and why do I need one? Test Strategy is documentation aligned with the test policy that describes the generic requirements for testing and details how to perform testing within an organization.

This documented approach lays out key types of testing needed and how you plan on addressing it. It is the test approach and guidelines you and your company must follow to assure a quality product.

If you are new to software testing many of these key terms are new to you. Within this series, we will bold new key terms that are relevant to software testing and define them.

Many official testing-related definitions are provided by ISTQB and other reputable sources. We will take these standard definitions and expand on key areas throughout this series.

Software is the entire set of programs, procedures, and related documentation associated with a mechanical or electronic system and especially a computer system.

Testing is the process consisting of all lifecycle activities, both static and dynamic, concerned with planning, preparation, and evaluation of a component or system and related work products to determine that they satisfy specified requirements, to demonstrate that they are fit for purpose, and to detect defects.

Software Testing is defined as an activity within Quality Control to check whether the actual results match the expected results and to ensure that the software system is defect or bug-free.

Scope

Identifying the scope of what you need to test is the first critical piece and lays the foundation for defining your test strategy. Think of the scope by identifying what product or service outcome is supposed to be in its ideal-finished state.

To properly set this test strategy, identify the business functions that must successfully be executed. Many business functions may span multiple applications or web services to accomplish that function.

You need to list all the applications that you need to incorporate into this test strategy.

Write them down and continue to reference them and the business functions as you think about detailing your test strategy.

Setting the scope lets you and your business know to what extent the software testing effort is covering.

If you are in a large organization, you may have one overall test strategy or policy which lays out key approaches for the entire QA organization but you also need detailed test strategies for each critical business function.

Chapter 2 – Test Management

Test Cases

Now that all the boring prep work is done, the fun begins! Most people that are software testers have a high level of curiosity and passion for breaking things! While it might seem like more fun to spend a majority of your time doing exploratory testing vs prep, prep does go a long way in improving your efficiency to validate and still meet the timeline demands you face.

Definition

Test Case - A set of preconditions, inputs, actions (where applicable), expected results and postconditions, developed based on test conditions.

Reasonability

Software Tester

Importance

Test cases are a critical part of software testing. Test cases hold the logical or process steps (preconditions) you have to take to execute the validation (postconditions). Test Cases are typically written in alignment with the requirements of the features in the software.

As you begin executing test cases, this is the moment in time that truly lets you see the quality level of the application. When you execute tests, it's a best practice to log the pass/fail results along with any **bugs** or **defects** found. Most companies track this effort in a test management tool or system.

Definition

Bug or Defect - An imperfection or deficiency in a work product where it does not meet its requirements or specifications.

Reasonability

Software Engineer

Importance

The logging of a bug or defect is critical to improving the quality of a product or service. This logging notifies the creator or supporter of the software code and allows them the chance to fix the issue. A resolution from the software engineer is required before you can validate the test case.

Traceability

Identifying how you are tracing back your test cases to the requirements needs to be included in your test strategy.

Traceability verifies all requirements are tested. One way to link the test cases to the requirements is by using a simple matrix. List all the requirements on one axis and list all the test cases on the other axis. Defining how you want to show traceability is what you need in your test strategy.

If you are including your test plan within your test strategy, be sure to spend enough time identifying all the requirements and mapping back to test cases within the matrix.

Requirements and Exit Criteria

Within your test strategy, you must lay out what pre-requisites you have before you can even execute tests. This might be something as simple as getting access to the application and/or getting a proper test data setup.

To complete the overall testing effort, you must identify what your exit criteria will be to be done. This should be similar to how you have exit criteria for each test case but at a higher level to say you are done with testing. This is a critical step to identify as testing efforts can drag on. It should tie back to the scope of the test strategy previously defined.

Defect Management

As your testing strategy gets defined and before you start prepping and execution, you must identify how you are going to track issues logged during execution.

Most large companies will have a separate tool to track test cases and defects in a test management system. Some of the more advanced companies will have this integrated into product backlogs or even code deployment tools. If not, at the very least you will want to leverage excel and some folders to log results and screenshots of any issues found.

You will need to share your results back with the developers to address any issues found.

The defect management part comes into play when developers indicate if the issue is a true defect or maybe not. Tracking this is critical so you don't waste time logging issues that were previously found.

Testing Environments

Many companies today have non-production environments that are used to "stage" applications for quality control. The larger the company the more testing environments are typically set up.

In your test strategy, you will want to identify <u>all your testing levels and testing types and indicate which non-production environment the test will be executed in.</u>

Testing Data

Test data is a critical piece to even execute a test. Your test strategy must account for how you plan on getting test data into the test environment and how it needs to be protected. Data protection and data privacy is a critical security approach that needs to be embedded into your test strategy.

For example, if you or your company stores credit card information or personally identifiable information, you must have a process to de-identify or mask sensitive information.

The larger the company the more integrated the test data needs are. Companies typically have a test data management practice that helps developers and testers get the test data they need and in a secured form.

Standard Tools

Identifying the tools used is critical to maintaining order and efficiency if you have a large testing organization.

At a minimum, you need to list all the types of testing that need to occur and the acceptable tools to leverage. A simple matrix will do.

Communication

Determine how, what, and when to communicate testing progress should be in your test strategy.

Come up with a standard template that shows overall test case and defect metrics. Showing how many test cases have been executed vs the number remaining shows clarity on how much effort is still needed. Also, show the defect status is critical for the development team so they know if they need to research and resolve it.

Try to leverage as much automation as possible as some of these metrics to be communicated can be loaded into dashboards or other tools.

Chapter 3 – Increasing TMMi (Testing Maturity Model)

What is TMMi?

TMMi stands for Testing Maturity Model and is an industry-standard for assessing your organization or business level of maturity in software quality testing. Think of this as answering the question "How good am I testing and validating the quality of my product?".

There are a few organizations that specialize in assessing your software quality practice using TMMi method. This would require an outside assessment of your processes and tools. One thing to note is that to get an official assessment, the company has to use certified TMMi assessors.

Finding out your TMMi level is a solid step in finding out what you are good at, what needs to improve, and what are the next steps to get to the next level and improve your chances of getting the QA Advantage over your competitors.

One thing to point out is that when you get a TMMi assessment is complete across the entire company. If one department is at a higher level of maturity than another department; the official level assigned is at the lower level. All departments across an organization must be at the same level.

In the next section, you will learn about the different TMMi levels and what are some of the activities your company or startup must complete being considered at that level.

Levels Defined

Level 1

Initial – This is the lowest level of maturity a company can have. If you do not have any formal quality assurance or testing practices.

Level 2

Managed – Where the fundamental test approach is established and managed. Your organization has test policies and standards, does test planning, test monitoring, test execution, test reporting, and proper test environment(s).

Level 3

Defined – Everything in the previous TMMi levels, in addition to a testing organization/center of excellence, testing training program, testing lifecycle, non-functional testing, and peer reviews.

Level 4

Measured – Everything in the previous TMMi levels, in addition to a test measurement and metrics program, product quality evaluation, and advanced reviews.

Level 5

Optimization – Everything in the previous TMMi levels, in addition to defect prevention, test process optimization, and automation, and quality control (highest level of production quality).

Assessment

You are likely wondering well how do I figure out what level I am at? The process is pretty straightforward. You have two choices. Either get officially certified at a TMMi level by an external organization or create an internal assessment.

External

If you are looking to be officially certified by TMMi; you must contact a company that can assess your level across the entire company. A simple web search for TMMi assessor will do.

Internal

Some companies prefer to do a customized approach to identifying their testing maturity and do their internal assessment. This can get similar results if you are not worried about getting officially registered and you have resources that have a high level of quality assurance and testing background. This is also a good step you can take to improve your levels before getting an external party involved. You can find someone in your organization that has the greatest breadth of quality assurance and testing knowledge to begin putting together an assessment question template.

Once assessments are completed, you are on the home stretch to improve your QA advantage.

This assessment is your playbook on what it takes to improve to the level of maturity within your company.

Please remember that if you are part of a larger company, each department will likely be at different maturity levels. To properly assess, you can have each department complete the assessment (external or internal) and come up with a more personalized action plan to improve and get to the next level.

Chapter 4 – Quality Improvement Process and Action Plans

Recap

If you have read the prior chapter on TMMi and decided to complete an assessment of your testing practice, this is the following step you should take. You will want to deep-dive into what it will take to get to the next testing maturity level.

Improvement Process and Action Plans

Organizations or startups that write down their quality improvement process and action plans have the greatest likelihood of successfully getting the QA advantage. Assigning a key quality leader resource to each department and having them partner with the assigned leadership for that department is key. This quality leader help drives the conversation on how the department can improve and gets agreement on action plans.

The action plan document can be as simple as a spreadsheet of what the improvement is, what is the priority, the timeline, and who is accountable for making it happen. Quality is not owned by one person; it is typically an entire team that needs to agree on the action plan. This will increase your likelihood of gaining a QA advantage over competitors.

Chapter 5 – Service Virtualization

What is Service Virtualization?

Service virtualization is a concept used during software development and testing. **In simplest terms, the developer or tester is trying to simulate (near real-time) a request & response process to validate something.**

Service virtualization is better suited for more integration & performance type of tests. You can simulate response times and do negative test scenarios which give this concept an edge over just using mock or stub tests.

Large organizations are more likely to use due to multiple development teams. Each team can carry-forward with development & testing to "virtualize" their service calls for the teams that might behind in development, reducing bottlenecks.

What is Service-Oriented Architecture?

To understand what service virtualization is, you should be familiar with the service-orientated architecture. Service-orientated architecture is an architecture pattern on how an application should be developed.

In regards to the integration of service calls between functions within the same application or many applications. You typically have a "producer" of a service. This is a team that "owns" the service creation. Then you have a "consumer" of a service. This is the end-user or team that "uses" the service.

For example, you send a request to look up a friend in Facebook app. That friend's info (response) is then returned to the user completing a request & response process. The data is likely being transmitted in the form of a service call.

You request something to happen, then a response is given.

When to use

Many companies that are using service virtualization realize the best uses for when to use service virtualization for software testing. **As mentioned in the summary above, the best use for this is for unit, integration, and performance testing of the service.** This is typically done on the "virtual" service due to the fact the "real" service is not available or still not consumable yet.

It is not advised to try to use virtual services for testing during the business user acceptance testing phase as this setup & use are quite technical in nature.

In theory, tools will continue to advance to make more self-serviceable & user-friendly but still requires a good understanding of application architecture.

Why use Service Virtualization?

The biggest reason for using service virtualization is to save time and money by catching development errors early(shift-left). Finding these issues sooner in the software development life-cycle costs less to fix.

Another reason to adopt this concept is that many applications being developed or maintained today are built on service-level architecture. It is easier to bring down a service, fix the issue, retest with virtual version, release back to production, then notify your users.

Companies are even looking to leverage a virtual service in production to keep their main or critical applications running. They would flip a switch on a feature and behind the screen, use a virtual service might just keep most of the application running and not losing sales.

How do I use Service Virtualization?

Service virtualization needs the proper framework and tool setup to operate. It typically requires a front-end web portal or client tool & a backend processing server.

There are many tools in the market and depending on your use case, some tools might work out better than others. It is advised to define your use cases and score the capabilities of the tools on the market.

Leverage a consultant if you need too as some of the infrastructure & culture change can get a bit complex. It is a journey but can be quite rewarding if implemented correctly and help you secure the QA advantage.

Chapter 6 – Database Virtualization

What is Database Virtualization?

Data virtualization decouples the database layer that sits between the storage and application layers in the application stack.

If you are familiar with how database systems work, you typically have a physical form of a database located on a server. This physical copy can be quite large and take time to transfer data back and forth. Database virtualization takes that physical copy and "virtualizes" it so it can be easily consumed at a rapid pace.

Why Database Virtualization?

The speed of innovation and ability to adapt to rapidly changing market trends rests on the agility of your release cycle and the ability to quickly diagnose, triage, and fix errors. Database virtualization is the critical lever used by forward-thinking enterprises to provision production-quality data to dev and test environments on-demand or via APIs.

When to use

- **DevOps:** For teams that need to transform app-driven customer experiences, oftentimes everything is automated except for the data. Data virtualization enables teams to delivers production-quality data to enterprise stakeholders for all phases of application development.

- **ERP Upgrades:** Over half of all ERP projects run past schedule and budget. The main reason? Standing up and refreshing project environments is slow and complex. Data virtualization can cut complexity, lower TCO, and accelerate projects by delivering virtual data copies to ERP teams more efficiently than legacy processes.

- **Cloud Migration:** Data virtualization technology can provide a secure and efficient mechanism to replace TB-size datasets from on-premise to the cloud, before spinning up space-efficient data environments needed for testing and cutover rehearsal.

- **Analytics and Reporting:** Virtual data copies can provide a sandbox for destructive query and report design and facilitate on-demand, data access across sources for BI projects that require data integration (MDM, M&A, global financial close, etc.)

- **Backup and Production Support:** In the event of a production issue, the ability to provide complete virtual data environments can help teams identify the root cause and validate that any change does not cause unanticipated regressions.

Understanding the QA Advantage

- **Enterprise-Grade Distribution:** Provision lightweight virtual database copies in minutes (depending on the types and size of files) via UI or API that scale with your agile development goals.

- **Built for Scale:** Replicate data from production to non-production environments at scale, either on-premises or in the cloud for multiple instances. Teams can provision virtual databases as necessary without taxing storage.

- **Data Governance:** Put your InfoSec department at ease with data controls that govern who can do what, where, and when over specific datasets. When combining best-in-class security, consistent data-masking policies, and robust auditing, data Virtualization becomes a security asset.

- **Cost Savings:** Maximize testing throughput while minimizing storage use - Virtual Datasets provisioning, destruction, refresh, and rewind all provide new tools for application testers to maximize testing throughput with virtually no additional storage cost.

Chapter 7 – DevOps (QA Automation)

What is DevOps?

A compound of development (Dev) and operations (Ops), DevOps is the union of people, processes, and technology to continually provide value to customers.

Teams that adopt DevOps culture, practices, and tools become high-performing, building better products faster for greater customer satisfaction.

With DevOps comes the concept of Quality Gates. Quality gates are validation checks the build pipeline can take to make sure code and proper testing are "validated" to move to production.

Automation

Automation is the backbone of the framework to make DevOps successful. All organizations are driving relentlessly towards implementing and maturing DevOps practices due to the completive advantage it brings.

Taking this step further for a QA advantage is key. While most companies are focusing on delivering code to production as quickly as possible most think of quality and testing as an afterthought. Quality must be built-in to the DevOps process.

Please see the next quality-focused areas to see how to fit into your DevOps practice.

Security Testing (within Pipeline)

Security testing has taken center stage lately and is critical to define in your test strategy and DevOps pipeline. If you have experienced any data breaches, you will understand that this section of your test strategy is not to be taken lightly.

Security validation techniques are evolving at a rapid pace but we will cover 3 important areas that are consistent to include in the test strategy and DevOps Pipelines.

- **Penetration Testing** is a testing technique aiming to exploit security vulnerabilities (known or unknown) to gain unauthorized access. This activity should be heavily performed when launching a new product or service before GO LIVE.

- **Static Application Security Testing (SAST)** focuses on white box security testing. Requires source code and finds vulnerabilities earlier in the software development lifecycle. Fixing these bugs typically costs the least. This activity should be done on each migration of the codebase and ideally integrated with an automated fashion.

- **Dynamic Application Security Testing (DAST)** focuses on black-box security testing. Requires application to be running and finds vulnerabilities later in the software development lifecycle. Fixing these bugs typically costs more. This activity should be done on each migration of the application.

Performance Testing (within Pipeline)

When people first think of non-functional testing, they usually think of performance first. The reason for this is because many application non-functional issues can be identified within the performance testing umbrella.

Performance testing is testing to determine the performance efficiency of a component or system.

There are many types of performance-related tests and the approach to test those types should be <u>clearly defined in your test strategy and DevOps pipelines.</u>

- **Load** – A type of performance testing conducted to evaluate the behavior of a component or system under varying loads, usually between anticipated conditions of low, typical, and peak usage.

- **Volume** – A type of performance testing conducted to evaluate the behavior of a component or system with large volumes of data. Also considered "flood testing". To flood the system with data.

- **Stress** – A type of performance testing conducted to evaluate a system or component at or beyond the limits of its anticipated or specified workloads, or with reduced availability of resources such as access to memory or servers.

- **Endurance** – Testing to determine the stability of a system under a significant load over a significant time within the system's operational context.

Relentless Feedback and Improvement

Implementing DevOps and Quality gates is a great start to increase your likelihood of gaining a QA advantage over competitors but it's not the end.

Production-live monitoring is a key difference maker and having a quick turnaround fix time. Do not let your customers experience bugs in production without the following:

Communication to your customers

Setup a quick communication model to let them know of any known production issues. Being proactive before your customer sees the issue will reduce the likelihood the customer goes to your competitor. It installs and builds up trust with them.

Resolve quickly

As your communication plan is underway, resolve the issue as quickly as possible but do not introduce more risk/bugs trying to resolve. Fixing an issue with not properly regression testing is the fastest way to lose more customers. If they see more than 1 issue or repeating the same mistakes, they are 10 times more likely to go somewhere else for their needs even if they have been a loyal customer.

Chapter 8 – Quality Revenue Impacts

Overview

This chapter provides information on how quality-related practices could impact revenue. These are key quality areas of focus. Along with great areas to continue to apply capital investments and mature.

Testing Maturity

Testing maturity is a broad subject but we wanted to call out a couple of areas that have the greatest impact on revenue. As companies continue to mature their testing practices, software development costs are reduced by shifting the quality left in the development lifecycle. What we mean by this is that the earlier your company finds an issue or defect in the code, the cheaper it is to fix.

Now taking this a step further left would be to make sure your company is documenting requirements in an agile fashion. This can catch design issues before any design or coding that needs to take place, possibly saving you thousands or even millions in a failed software product or service launch.

It is recommended that your company leverages an agile software development approach to quickly adapt to customer needs while reducing any wasteful software development.

As your company matures in agile methodology, your testing maturity is also maturing and rapidly enhancing outdated practices. Your testing organization will influence how the entire software development organization will mature and executive leaders will begin to inject more capital funding as they see proper products being built efficiently.

Automation

It is no secret that automation drives a consistent result. This is critical to quality best practices. If your organization can automate much of the software development and release cadence, quality checks can be automated and failsafe's can be instituted with minimal human interaction.

Data shows that the costliest issues or defects in a production environment are due to some human or environment setup error. Removing as many steps that touch the human hand will set up a repeatable practice that can be scaled enterprise-wide. This will reduce costly fixes needed due to human error.

Continue to invest in scaling a modern development pipeline with quality built-in to the process.

Setup quality gates that check for proper environment setup and/or configurations, code is deployed, and testing execution has been completed before moving to production. All of which can be mostly automated. Leverage your testing experts or business users as a final validation if needed, but even then, the human interaction should be minimal.

QA Innovation

The area of innovation can be difficult to invest in as it requires the notion that capital expenses spent are likely to fail. That might be true but some of the most successful companies are set up this way.

Many large organizations are trying to catch up and shift culture into a test-n-learn organization which allows more of the start-up entrepreneur mentality to organically grow.

Innovation in the QA space is following the same approach for trying out new technologies and see how your business can adopt those. Quality-related tools and new processes are being matured daily.

Many large companies such as IBM, Microsoft, and HP are realizing they need to invest in linking software development and quality engineering practices to secure those big sales contracts.

Technology is rapidly changing and the best organizations realize that they need to invest in a test-n-learn approach and use data analytics to drive product innovations. This is a similar approach that is needed for quality assurance and engineering.

Quality assurance departments need to focus on their internal customers on how can my department innovate to want to improve the quality practice.

Quality leaders are focusing on taking new technologies and influencing key decision-makers in areas such as data engineering, cognitive/analytics, and enterprise transformation. Those folks in quality assurance engineering understand how they can take a new technology and reduce company costs.

For example, maybe your test data security & availability has been a challenge for some time. Software engineering and software testers need access to test data in real-time.

Investing in data engineering and tech innovation proof-of-technology concepts will drive innovation and likely reduce large company expenses if properly conducted.

If not, hopefully, you have set up a test-n-learn culture that reduces unneeded waste while you continue to invest in successful QA innovation.

Conclusion

Over time… software development and testing best practices evolve, keeping current with new technology and knowing how to test them is always a challenge.

Knowing how to build quality into your processes and improving those is how you will gain the QA advantage over your competitors.

More Info

Over time... software development and testing best practices evolve, keeping current with new technology and knowing how to test them is always a challenge.

The software testing community is expanding rapidly and becoming more specialized. This requires an open mind to see what is possible and challenge what's possible to assure software testing is keeping up with technology changes.

The mindset of being a software tester is consistent and strong over the decades, technology is not. Learn the basics and then expand. Have a solid background on key software testing concepts and communicating those best practices to key assuring stakeholders.

My hope is this book will help new and current software testers navigate the world of software testing. Not only advancing your knowledge in software testing but also enable options into broader software quality management best practices or educate others.

The opportunity to enhance yourself are endless. You can focus on broad quality management which covers assurance and control or specialize in a particular area within quality control (i.e. software testing). Only you can determine which path you would like to go!

If you enjoyed this book on software quality, please stay connected as we release future books on software quality.

Further Reference

The creation of this book is in partnership with Apply QA, LLC; a leading provider of best practices and consultation services for modern software quality assurance, engineering, innovation, and control.

Please visit https://applyqa.com to check out further information on the subject.

Other References

ISTQB Glossary https://glossary.istqb.org/en/search/

Merriam-Webster https://www.merriam-webster.com/dictionary/software